Where is My Honey?

T0123273

Where is My Honey?

AILSON J. DE MORAES

authorHOUSE®

AuthorHouse™ LLC
1663 Liberty Drive
Bloomington, IN 47403
www.authorhouse.com
Phone: 1-800-839-8640

Published by AuthorHouse 09/25/2014

ISBN: 978-1-4969-3057-6 (sc)
ISBN: 978-1-4969-3058-3 (e)

Library of Congress Control Number: 2014914917

Praise for 'Where is My Honey?'

A SIMPLE TALE ABOUT ACHIEVING OUR GOALS AND AMBITIONS BY ADAPTING OUR CIRCUMSTANCES IN LIFE

"This book is unique, in the sense that it is simple to understand but holds a powerful message. I highly recommend this book if anyone wants a simple insight into leadership and motivation. Read this book!"

--- Crystal Ho, Risk Consultant
KPMG, Hong Kong

"Fantastically thought provoking and an absolute recipe for successful leadership and professional development!"

--- Lee Wetherilt, CEO
ING Group, UK

"This accessible and thought-provoking story reminds us of the links between the values of teamwork, hard-work and leadership.

I found it both inspiring and beneficial, and shall be using it to convey its positive message to others."

--- Dr Chris Bonnici
University of Malta

"This book is simple and easy to read yet it has a powerful message.
Read this book!"

--- Shady H. Diab, Engagement Executive Manager Fawry for banking and payment technology services, Egypt

"It is a very short piece of writing packed with lots of gems. Well done!"

Zach Anucha, Information Security Auditor Consultant, NCC Group, UK

"A great story! I enjoyed reading it! It was a pleasant way to learn about leadership. I agree that leaders can be made."

--- Laura Migenda
Deloitte, Switzerland

"It's an amazing book! Suitable for people of all ages. An exciting and interesting way of showing all the leadership skills and qualities hidden in every person and the opportunities for developing them that shouldn't be missed.
It makes its reader realize they shouldn't just live their lives as it comes, but take matters in their own hands.
Amazing book! Congratulations!"

--- Neli Mihaylove,
Business Student, UK

"The story of Belinda Bee opens the eyes for one to think within and without the box. It explains the reason as to why a leader needs to build a team, work hard and ask for help when one is overwhelmed. It makes the whole concept to look simple and memorable. It can be read at a sitting.

Ailson J. De Moraes

It is a powerful motivational tool!"

--- **William Munga**
Kenya Literature Bureau, Kenya

"I found this book very interesting and inspirational; in fact it's not the usual book one would find on the shelves about leadership, which is often boring. This book tells an interesting story which relates not only to leadership and personal qualities, but also putting your mind to something and you can achieve it. The fact that the book is enjoyable to read, means that you remember the story and pick out the key messages in the book. The book was very clear and easy to read throughout, and it ends with a strong motivational message."

--- **Giancarlo Mortellaro**
Milia Living Home, Italy

"This book is simple and easy to read yet it has a powerful message. Read this book!"

--- **Iara Amaral**
Lawyer, Brazil

"It's been said that the best way to teach is through a story and this book re-emphasizes my believe in the saying. The quality and yet simple words in use are a testament to the author's intelligent thinking, the easy read of the book cuts across all age groups.

The message is simple and clear; 'the limit to what we can achieve is in our mind'.

Thank you Ailson for the encouragement within this rich book."

--- Hannah Fredrick
Legalframes, UK

"This is a very good and easy read for all ages. This is a book that business leaders, adults from all walks of life and children can benefit from. It contains a good combination of hints of leadership, management and sometimes religious principles. Students of Leadership as well as Strategic Management would find some applications of theoretical principles."

--- Dr Ellis Luther Osabutey
Middlesex University, UK

"Short and easy book to read with lots to learn from it. Great examples on leadership. Read it, you will enjoy it!"

--- Kam Sethi, Executive Consultant Deloitte, UK

"This book sends out a powerful message for any aspiring leader to be: Where there is a will, there is a way!"

Romina Iro Savvopoulou Postgraduate Student at London School of Economics

"I found the story very insightful, yet very easy to read and understand and what's more important to remember the lessons this little bee has learnt. I think the book will have readers of different age, not only adults but even children may get interested if the story could be introduced like an animated cartoon film (when reading I could clearly imagine Belinda buzzing around in an attempt to find a sound and effective solution)."

--- Irma Patsia Professional in the Oil Industry, Georgia

"I read your book with great interest, a small book yet packed with so many key concepts.

I lost my job since November 2011, and I realized that I needed help to think things through, and your book just did this. If I had to select only 2 key-concepts among many that are empowering me right now, these are the ones I found in this book: 1- The crisis brings the opportunity, and 2- The solution is already in the problem. Now I am going to unpack this in my personal situation and see where it leads me as I have decided a Career Transition.

Thanks again Ailson for sharing these life-empowering insights."

--- Albert Podorski
Unemployed (not for long!), Portugal

"'Where is my honey' nailed it on point! The book gives plenty priceless lessons to learn in life. The essential 'skills' of a leader are balance, flexibility, creativity and observation. Sometimes the transformation of an individual can lead to the revolution of the whole group. Everyone can be a leader just like everyone can be a cook but to be an excellent one, hidden skills are the one that make the differences. You will have to accept the challenges and the fact that some people

will make it difficult for you to achieve your goal. Be upset and move on, then replace the negativity with confidence and patience.

The book gives plenty priceless lessons to learn in life.

What a recipe of success!"

Giun Milo
University Student, UK

"The helpful principles that have been placed at the end of the chapters really help me to draw upon the advice when I need it the most. I hope to put into practice the experienced advice you have provided!"

--- Ashutosh Taunk
IT Entrepreneur, India

Help your people to find their 'honey' and build a truly successful organization

FOR MORE INFORMATION
ON KEYNOTE SPEECHES AND
SEMINARS GO TO
WWW.WHEREISMYHONEY.COM

About the Author

I am a privileged man. My life journey thus far has been one of adventure and rich life experiences; from leaving my native homeland of Brazil to Europe at the age of 20 to becoming a respected international university teacher, author, entrepreneur and international speaker. As an international speaker, I have been given talks on the topics of leadership and personal development to a variety of audience, from speaking to executives, professional teachers, young minds, teenagers and even primary school teachers and students, I feel being welcomed in any age group of creative minds anywhere in the world. Speaking three main international languages I have been able to reach literally thousands of individuals in four continents. My main goal: to encourage and assist you to make the best of your life. Remember, life is a journey and you are the captain of your life-journey, it is you who decide the destination!

My work has taken me to many wonderful places around the world and I have met thousands of individuals on their own life journeys of self-discovery and in pursuit of an extraordinary life. I have been able to learn so many interesting life stories from individuals (people like you and me) from so many different backgrounds and I thank to everyone who kindly shared his/her own life story with me. My own personal experience tells me that provided that you have a health mind you can literally achieve absolutely amazing things in your life -*'anybody can become extraordinary'*, it's only a matter of *focus* and *determination*.

In this little powerful book, I am writing not only a simple tale of Belinda the Bee (yes, she is actually a bee!), I am literally telling the story of many people around the planet, people like you and me. People who are making the most of their lives. Do you want to be part of this group? Read the book and reflect in your personal and professional life. Drop me a line – www.whereismyhoney.com tell me and the world what lessons you can learn from Belinda the Bee. After reading this short parable, how will you plan to act in your life?

Over the years it became clear to me that mediocrity is just not enough for many of us; and that single revelation was the driving force behind this book. Through my many years of teaching literally thousands of people from all over the world I have found that there are many people, like you and me, seeking a way out of the mundane routines we often allow ourselves to slide into. We become too comfortable and complacent. We close our inner ears to the desire deep down inside that's screaming for more. Do you want more from your life? Do you want to live an extraordinary life? Read the book and reflect in your wants and desires.

WHY WRITING THIS BOOK?

It's a well-known fact that most people learn better through parables or stories. Pairing this knowledge with my desire to help those seeking to live an extraordinary life, I began to develop *Where Is My Honey?* This thought-provoking tale is about the very ordinary, Belinda the Bee and her path of discovering her full potential. Hidden within this simple story lies a powerful message for all who desire to not just accept the life laid before them, but who wish to gain the tools needed to take charge of their destinies.

"It's been said that the best way to teach is through a story and this book re-emphasizes my belief in the saying. The quality and yet simple words in use are a testament to the author's intelligent

thinking, the easy read of the book cuts across all age groups.

The message is simple and clear; 'the limit to what we can achieve is in our mind'.

Thank you Ailson for the encouragement within this rich book."

--- Hannah Fredrick, UK.

There has never been a better time to take your first step towards the extraordinary, and I thank you for allowing me the honor of taking it with you. Now, on to the adventure ahead…

Where is My Honey?

A Simple Tale about Achieving Our Goals and

Ambitions by Adapting Our Circumstances in Life

Visit the Website

www.whereismyhoney.com

AILSON J. DE MORAES

Dedicated to all amazing people I have met around the world. You are wonderful! You are my inspiration and mission! Its an honor and privilege to serve and support you!

Thank you for allowing me to be part of your life. This book is for you!

"Only those who will risk going too far can possibly find out how far one can go."
—*T. S. Eliot*

This tale is based on a true story – my own personal life story!

Visit my personal website
www.ailsondemoraes.com

Contents

Bees are hard workers! 'Dreams become reality through hard work.'

We have no food! The entire hive is in disarray! No one knows what to do! – 'EACH OF US IS BORN WITH THE POTENTIAL TO DO GREAT THINGS.'

Belinda needed time to think. Aimlessly flying through the dark, she felt fear surrounding her like a giant net, capturing her mind and making it hard for her to think creatively as she tried to come up with a plan to save the hive. 'Fear blocks the mind and makes it harder to think creatively.'

Belinda and General Hardwork wasted no time getting their workers assembled into their different groups of ants and bees, sending each combined group to set strategic locations that had the highest likelihood of success. 'Group work, the secret of real success.'

If Belinda was honest and realistic, she had to face the fact that the honey-shortage problem had not been properly solved after all. 'BEING HONEST AND REALISTIC = QUALITIES OF GOOD LEADERS.'

Belinda realized that if she wanted to find a solution, she was going to have to start thinking outside of the box, broaden her perspective, and approach the problem from different angles. 'Are you thinking outside of the box?'

As Belinda surveyed the end results of her plan, she was proud of the hive and everything they had accomplished together. 'When you look at the results in your life, do you feel proud of everything you have accomplished?'

Belinda surveyed the end results of her plan, and she she was proud of the hive and everything they and they had accomplished together.

To reward everyone for the hard work done, Belinda organized a huge feast for the next day. 'Reward everyone for the hard work done, including your own, is extremely important and relevant to move on in life.'

The End of the Beginning.

This is My Story.…..

Characterization

The imaginary characters presented in this story are intended to reveal to us the simple and complex pars of ourselves when facing challenges in our everyday life, regardless of our age, gender, racial, cultural or nationality background.

Honey is a metaphor for what you want or wish in life – whether it is more money, a better job, a loving relationship, health or spiritual peace of mind, anything that can make you a better person. The garden in the story is the closest community in your life; it is the place where most things happen around. The hive is the organization you work, the school or university you study in, your family or the local community you live in. However, you are very welcome to interpret what can be your honey, garden and your hive according to your own understanding and necessity. Use your creative mind and explore the story to learn more about you and your community around.

Belinda:

Belinda is a hardworking little bee, working hard from early in the mornings till late in the afternoon. She was merely a humble nectar collector, but in her heart she yearned to accomplish more with her life. She wanted to be more than a mere nectar collector, but her own fears and beliefs were holding her back. However, when life intervened she was forced out of her comfort zone, and had to grow as the situation required. Learning from others, she developed the potential she already had and started growing into the bee she always dreamed of being.

David:

David is the managing director of a large manufacturing company. Since life can sometimes become very stressful at work, he likes to come home in the afternoon and relax in his garden. Even though he is very successful in his professional life, he is humble, and treats everybody with respect. He doesn't look down on Belinda because she is a bee; instead he befriended her and always tries to help where he can.

The Queen Bee:

During times of prosperity The Queen is generally not a bad leader, but as most leaders, she still has to learn a few things about leadership before she will be an effective leader. During times of crises The Queen can't be relied on by the hive, and looks to her subjects to save them from the lurking danger. She still has to learn the importance of prioritizing tasks in accordance to importance and urgency. She has to learn how to delegate less important tasks, to strategize, and so forth.

She does, however, encourage Belinda to use her leadership talents in this important task. She is happy when Belinda steps forward and tries to make a plan to save the hive which in the end resulted in a successful plan.

The Bee Farmer:

The bee farmer is a short tempered, self-conceited, and very selfish man. He has no regard for anyone but himself. He believes he is superior to the bees and therefore can do as he pleases, and take honey whenever it pleases him. He has no compassion for the bees and treats them as his slaves.

General Ant Hardwork:

General Hardwork is the commanding officer of the ant's military forces, and is also the right-hand ant of the Ant Queen. He is a hardworking Ant, and a brilliant strategizer. He is always drawing up plans to improve on the offensive and defensive strategies of the anthill. He works well with others, and is not scared to tackle a seemingly impossible problem. He has a well of information gained by experience, and always tries to help others, sharing his knowledge and experience, helping them to grow. He is a leader in his own way.

The Bee Population:

The bees at hive nr.54 are all hardworking bees, but have become so comfortable in their circumstances and daily routine, that no one was prepared or mentally equipped to handle the honey crises when it happened. They buzzed around in terror, fearing for the worst, unable to lead themselves out of the crises. They don't have the power to think for themselves, they need a leader to take control and lead them in the direction they needed to go. They really understand teamwork and accept the fact that good teams need good leaders.

The Ants:

The ants are a well-organized, hard working group of individuals. Everything had an order to it, and everyone knew what was expected of them and what to do to achieve their objective. They share the responsibility of the work in the nest and help each other where they can. They have a one for all and all for one, type of philosophy. They get on well with others and understand the principal of teamwork, and what can be accomplished through it.

Whatever stage of our lives we are, we all share something in common: *a need to find our 'honey' and succeed in changing times.* In the end of the day, we are all the same; *we are all humans looking for 'honey' in life.*

Enjoy the reading!

The Story Behind the Story of "Where is My Honey?"

The Story of *Where is My Honey ?* was created first of all to help me to deal with my own understanding of the human potential. I created this story based on my own life experience which shows me that anyone can become extraordinary with the right determination and focus in life. The story shows that by working with our potential we can become someone we have never imagined to be; and this is my own personal life story. More about my life story, check out on my personal website www.ailsondemoraes.com

We all have dormant potential, but finding a way to unlock that potential is where our limitations lie. *Where is My Honey* is the story of a simple bee, happy in the world as she knows it, yet keen for something more. When tragedy hits and the bees face imminent death it falls to Belinda the bee to find a solution.

Is this too big a challenge for her? Or could this be the push she needs to reveal her true, leading character?

Not only is this story a refreshing and entertaining read, but it offers guidance; teaching us all how to make the most of our skills and potential and ultimately be proud of our own individuality.

People who have read the first manuscript revealed that the story of Belinda the bee can be identified with some stages of their own lives. The story of Belinda the bee has improved their leadership skills, personal confidence, career plans, businesses perspectives, and even their personal relationships. I am glad to be able to 'serve' you with *'Where is My Honey.'*

I invite you too to reflect on the story of Belinda the bee, and to interpret and apply it to your own situation that gives it value. It is my sincerely hope that you interpret the tale of *Where is My Honey?* by putting it into action in your own life, and identify *'Where is YOUR Honey'* that you deserve. Good luck!

"Where is My Honey? is an enlightening and inspiring read...simple yet powerful. It captures the daily trials we face when working in a competitive and diverse world. Shaping our leadership skills takes guts, and this short story proves that we have the capability to lead, it has always been there, all we need to do is reach out...take it and own it."

--- **Joanna Seraspi, Accenture**

"Fantastically thought provoking and an absolute recipe for successful leadership and professional development!"

--- **Lee Wetherilt, CEO, ING Group, UK**

"This book is simple and easy to read yet it has a powerful message.

9

Read this book!"

--- **Shady H. Diab, Fawry for banking and payment technology services, Egypt**

"The message is simple and clear; 'the limit to what we can achieve is in our mind'. Thank you Ailson for the encouragement within this rich book."

--- **Hannah Fredrick, Legalframes, UK**

HAVING DREAMS
OF A BETTER
LIFE MAKES
YOU HAPPY

by Karl Da Silva

Episode One

Like many of us, Belinda Bee was a hard-working bee. Every morning at dawn she would head out looking for nectar and pollen, and she would return back to the hive when the sun went down, just plain exhausted from a long day of work. Some days she was lucky and found nectar close to the hive. Other days she would have to fly far, far away to collect only the tiniest bit of pollen from far-off fields.

One day Belinda headed out in search for nectar just as she had done every morning of her working life. As she rushed out of the hive, she passed the honey tasters who were enjoying a relaxed cup of honey before work. The sight of them filled Belinda with envy, and she left the hive feeling extremely unhappy with her life. Oh, she knew that she had a fairly important job for which she should be grateful; but in her heart she yearned to accomplish more. She wanted more out of life than what she was getting. She dreamed of a better life, of being a respected individual in the bee society, and of living a comfortable, fulfilling existence. She was tired of settling for mediocrity. She wanted to move past the current boundaries of her day-to-day world and reach for the stars. But, like so many of us, she was held back by her fears, convinced that her dream was just unattainable.

Thoroughly depressed, Belinda buzzed half-heartedly along from one garden to the next, ruminating. She wished that there was some way she could change her life and become the bee she yearned to be. The more she thought about everything, the more depressed she became. But she just couldn't believe that she could rise above her circumstances and attain the life she had always dreamed of having. She just hadn't been born with the right set of skills to be more than a humble and ordinary bee, or so she thought…

> *"HAVING DREAMS OF*
>
> *A BETTER LIFE MAKES*
>
> *YOU HAPPY."*

Episode Two

That evening Belinda returned to the hive, only to be shocked at the utter chaos that met her. Her fellow bees were buzzing hither and thither in a total state of panic.

"What's going on? What happened?" Belinda asked one of the guards near the entrance of the hive.

"We're all going starve!" the guard exclaimed in a panic.

"What do you mean? I don't understand."

"The farmer collected the honey earlier than normal! He took most of the honey! He's left us with almost no food!" The guard began to weep, completely beside himself with fear.

"The farmer took all of the honey? But why'd he do that? How are we going to feed everyone if there is no honey?!" The magnitude of the catastrophe began to tighten its grip on Belinda.

"That's not the worst of it!" The guard's eyes were wide with fright. "The larvae is hatching within the next seven days! They will all die if there's nothing to eat!" He buzzed off in state of panic.

"This is a disaster," Belinda said to herself, finding a path through the chaos. She couldn't begin to imagine what their immediate future looked like—it was too horrible to even picture!

Belinda stood in the center of the hive and watched in shock as everyone buzzed wildly in circles, too blind with terror to think logically about the situation. The longer Belinda watched, the more overwhelming became her concern for the wellbeing of the hive. Suddenly, she realized that someone needed to take control and restore order to the hive. It was clear that the hive wasn't capable of leading itself! She knew that buzzing about in panic was not going to solve their problem. She had an irresistible desire to restore order. The bees needed someone to lead them— someone had to come up with a solution to their problem.

The queen! How could I forget? Belinda felt relief wash over her. As their leader, the queen would know what to do! Hope was burning high in her heart as she rushed off to speak to the queen.

Arriving at the royal egg chamber, Belinda found the queen busy laying a new batch of eggs. Belinda kneeled elegantly in front of her.

"My Queen, I'm sorry to disturb you, but the hive is in complete chaos. We need you to take control!" Even Belinda's great respect and restraint could not conceal her distress.

"Yes, I am aware of what is going on. The farmer has really created a huge problem for us," the queen answered, momentarily pausing in her task. "I just don't know what to do," she admitted, her eyes clouded with fear. "It is impossible for me to cease laying eggs midway through the process."

"But, my Queen, we have no food! The entire hive is in disarray! No one knows what to do!" Belinda was perplexed at the queen's unwillingness to take control of her kingdom and address the situation.

"I understand the magnitude of the problem, but, as you can see, I'm completely occupied," the queen sighed heavily. She then fixed Belinda with a direct stare. "Belinda, I need you to step in for me. You must take control of the hive and find a solution to our problem."

"What? Me? But I don't know the first thing about leading a hive!" Belinda shook her head in disbelief.

> # "EACH OF US IS
> # BORN WITH THE POTENTIAL
> # TO DO GREAT THINGS."

"Belinda, each of us is born with the potential to do great things. Most of us never get to use or discover that potential because we never find ourselves in a situation where life demands it of us. Life in our hive has now changed in a most unfortunate manner. This will demand more from all of us. We will have to move out of our comfort zones and grow along with our new circumstances. We can only hope that in the process we will develop and become better than what we used to be." The queen was most solemn and forthright. "Belinda, instead of losing your self to panic and buzzing around with your fellow bees, you came here in search of a solution. That indicates to me that you have heaps of untapped potential just waiting to be uncovered. You are a diamond in the rough. You are on the verge of being cut and polished—and you will shine!

I believe in you! I know you won't let me down! Now, go forth! Lead the hive! Find the solution to our problem."

"I will do as you ask, my Queen. I will do my best not to let you down." Belinda backed out of the chamber in a daze. How in the world she was going to be able to fulfill such an enormous promise?

> *"Effective leaders are those who make their followers aware of their capacities, and give them the authority to take appropriate action when an opportunity challenges them."*
>
> *---Leaders make other leaders!---*
>
> *—The Queen Bee*

Episode Three

The responsibility and magnitude of her task weighed heavily on Belinda as she left the queen behind in the royal egg chamber. She was only one little bee. How on earth was she going to lead the hive and save them from starvation?

Feeling the panic of the hive closing in on her, Belinda zoomed out into the cool evening air. She needed time to think. Aimlessly flying through the dark, she felt fear surrounding her like a giant net, capturing her mind and making it hard for her to think creatively as she tried to come up with a plan to save the hive.

> **'Fear blocks the mind and makes it harder to think creatively.'**

It wasn't long before Belinda realized that she was getting nowhere on her own. She needed help. In her daily work, she had become a frequent visitor to the garden of a man named David. Over time the two of them had become good friends. Perhaps David would be able to give her some perspective and help her come up to with a solution.

We all need time to think

"ASKING FOR HELP

IS OK."

Arriving at David's home, Belinda headed straight for the window that opened to the living room, where she knew she would find him spending time with his family.

"Oh, hi there, Belinda. This is a pleasant surprise!" David smiled warmly at Belinda as she landed on the coffee table in front of him.

"Hi there, David. I hope I'm not disturbing you." Belinda glanced around to see where David's family was, but he was alone.

"No, not in the least," David answered. "To what do I owe the honor of your visit?"

"I came to ask your advice. Disaster has struck the hive, and now I'm sitting with a colossal problem which I don't know how to solve." Belinda went on to explain everything that had happened.

"Wow, that really is a disaster!" David's eyes were full of concern for his little friend. "The only thing I can suggest is that you go and explain the severity of your situation to the farmer. I'm sure that once he understands the magnitude of your problem, he'll be willing to come to an agreement with you and return some of the honey."

"That's a great idea!" Belinda looked as if a crown of excitement had been perched on her head. "I don't know why I didn't think of it in the first place!"

"Don't be too hard on yourself. Sometimes you can stand too close to a problem and miss the most obvious solution!"

After spending a couple of minutes discussing this and that, Belinda bade goodbye to David and headed back to the hive to get a good night's sleep. She wanted to be well rested and refreshed for her important meeting with the farmer the next morning.

> ## "<u>REST</u> IS VITAL FOR <u>BODY</u> AND <u>MIND</u>."

Episode Four

Belinda was up early the next morning, filled with a mixture of fear and excitement. Nervous energy surged through her tiny body while she readied herself for her meeting with the farmer. Everyone knew that the farmer was a short-tempered man who hated to be interrupted while he was working. In fact, in the past he had actually killed a couple of bees who had dared to interrupt him. But Belinda felt that she didn't have a choice; she simply had to take the risk. Even though she might lose her life, she had to muster up the nerve to approach the farmer and convince him to come to an agreement and return some of the honey. Gathering all of her courage, Belinda left to face him.

"Take Risks"

On her way out of the hive, she couldn't help but notice that her fellow bees seemed a lot calmer that morning, with everything in the hive slowly returning to its old rhythm and routine. The news that the queen had appointed Belinda to take control of the situation and find a solution seemed to have given everyone the reassurance they needed to continue with their daily tasks.

Flying up into the daylight, Belinda could see the farmer in the distance, busy removing honey from another hive. I can do this, Belinda kept repeating to herself. She formed a clear vision of what she wanted to accomplish and imagined a positive reaction from the farmer. Pulling all of her pluck together, Belinda flew up to the farmer, and landed on top of the hive where he was working.

"Good morning, Sir, how are you this morning?" Belinda greeted the farmer with the biggest smile she could muster.

"Good morning." The farmer was annoyed already.

"Sir, my name is Belinda Bee. I live at hive nr.54— you know, the big hive next to the cherry tree," Belinda stammered. The farmer's clear irritation with her presence was throwing her off her game a bit. It was becoming harder for her to continue envisioning anything positive emerging from this meeting.

"Yes, how can I help you?" The farmer pointedly looked at his watch. He clearly wanted to get back to work.

"Well, Sir, yesterday you arrived ahead of schedule and removed most of the honey from our hive." Belinda nervously twisted her antennae together.

**Clear Vision is the KEY to
an EXTRAordinary LIFE**

"So? What's the problem?" the farmer asked impatiently.

"The problem is that you've collected honey out of schedule. Now we don't have any food for the group of larvae that's about to hatch." Reminded of her plight, Belinda answered clearly and directly, her fear and nervousness giving way to confidence and determination.

> ## *"FEAR* and *NERVOUSNESS* CAN be replaced with <u>CONFIDENCE</u> and <u>DETERMINATION</u>."

"And what do you expect me to do about it?" The farmer snorted, snatching his bee smoker up from the ground.

"Sir, I was hoping that we could come to some mutually beneficial agreement," Belinda explained more confidently, keeping her vision crystal clear in her mind. "If you will agree to return thirty percent of the honey that you took yesterday, then we will agree to give you an extra ten percent of our half of the honey for the next six months."

"You're only a bee. I don't negotiate with bees," the farmer said, staring down his nose at Belinda. "You come here to bargain with me as if I need your permission to take whatever honey I want from the hive? If you're not careful, I'll take all of your honey every week and not leave you a drop! Now get away from me! I've got a lot of work to do!" He blew his smoker at Belinda, enveloping her in a suffocating haze.

Coughing, and with burning eyes, Belinda fled, with the farmer's laughter following her all the way. This was terrible! She had failed! She couldn't understand why he was so unwilling to come to an agreement. Wasn't her proposal alluring enough? Was that why he had been so hostile? And why didn't he negotiate with bees?

Belinda was filled with questions and hopelessness. She had failed with the farmer and she failed to save the hive. What was she going to do now? How was she supposed to save the hive? Not yet ready to face the hive and admit to her failure, Belinda flew to a nearby stream and alighted on a yellow flower. There was no way she could go home without an alternative plan. She wasn't willing to give up and admit defeat. She was determined to see the problem through to the end and somehow come up with a solution.

DETERMINATION = SOLUTION

SOLUTION = SUCCESS

SUCCESS = FULFILLMENT

Episode Five

Sitting next to the stream, Belinda allowed her thoughts to flow with the water. Soon a multitude of weird and wonderful (if not always spectacular) ideas started streaming through her mind. As she was rejecting one idea after the other, Belinda saw two ants walking over the earth, carrying a large berry between them. While Belinda watched them help each other with the load, a proper, workable plan started to form in her mind.

Buzzing with excitement Belinda made her way to the ants' nest and asked the guards at the entrance if she could speak to their queen. After a couple of minutes, the guards returned to tell her that their queen was not available for interviews; however, Belinda could speak to their general if she wished. Relieved that the ants were willing to grant her any sort of audience at all, Belinda accepted their offer and was then led into the maze of tunnels that ran through the nest. The guards took Belinda to the operations chamber, where the general was busy going over defense strategies with a group of soldier ants.

"Good day, Sir, I'm Belinda. Thank you for taking the time to see me."

"Pleased to meet you, Belinda, I'm General Hardwork. Please take a seat," the general indicated where Belinda could sit. "I must say that I was very surprised when the guards told me that there was a bee here to see me," the general smiled.

"General, I've come here today to ask your help," Belinda said, her eyes pleading. She started to explain the whole situation to him.

"What a disaster!" the general exclaimed. "But why do you think that we can help you?"

"General, it's widely known that ants are hard workers and excellent food gatherers, while bees can quickly cover great distances and find food with relative ease."

> # "ANTS (and BEES) ARE HARD WORKERS, ARE YOU?"

Belinda continued, "With that in mind, I was hoping that we could combine our forces, locating and transporting nectar with greater speed, thus helping us to secure high volumes of nectar within a short period of time." Belinda went into detail about how the two communities could divide everyone into teams, with the bees locating the nectar sources, and the ants transporting the nectar. "To compensate you for the loss of working time during the collaboration, we will give you one milliliter of honey for every day you spend helping us," Belinda concluded with a bouncing heart, clearly imagining a positive outcome to her proposal.

"That sounds like a great plan," the general agreed, smiling as he thought of the sweet honey reward they would receive for their efforts.

"Thank you so much! I can't tell you how much I appreciate your willingness to help. If there's ever anything we can do to help you, please don't hesitate to ask," Belinda buzzed in jubilation.

Belinda and the general then started drawing up strategic plans for the merger of their forces. If there was one thing that the general knew how to do well, it was planning and strategizing. Belinda quickly picked up on this and paid careful attention to the way he approached the situation, and she noted his reasoning behind each of his decisions. Deciding on the amount of workers needed for each task, the areas of land to be covered, and the different groups that the workers would be divided into, the two went over every aspect of their plan, discussing everything in the finest detail and leaving nothing to chance.

BE VISIONARY AND DETAILED = SUCCESSFUL LEADER

With the plan perfectly worked out, Belinda and the general each set off to make the necessary arrangements and preparations so that they could become fully operational early the next morning. Filled with pride, Belinda returned to the hive to share the good news with the queen and the rest of her fellow bees. In a formal meeting, Belinda shared her vision with the entire hive and made sure that they all knew exactly what was expected of them. Everyone in the hive was thrilled! With her energy and intricate details, she created quite a stir amongst her fellow bees, getting everyone hyped up and just as engrossed in her plans.

Taking what she had learned from the general, Belinda started dividing everyone into specific groups according to their talents and experience. Each group would have specific tasks to perform, which would utilize their talents and experience to the fullest. The hive was a hubbub of activity with everyone hurrying about and finishing all of the preparations before the next morning. Feeling more comfortable with her role as a leader, Belinda oversaw the different preparations and helped and advised her fellow bees whenever she could, empowering everyone with whom she came into contact. She had a good feeling about the plan and was becoming increasingly excited and impatient to become operational and save the hive.

Strategic and Effective Leaders Empower their followers.

At dawn the following morning, Belinda and her fellow bees set off to the anthill where the ants were ready and eager to help the bees to save their hive. Belinda and General Hardwork wasted no time getting their workers assembled into their different groups of ants and bees, sending each combined group to set strategic locations that had the highest likelihood of success.

With General Hardwork perched on her back, Belinda flew from one location to the next, happy to see the workers speedily helping each other to locate, collect, and transport the nectar back to the hive. By noon, Belinda was astounded by the sheer volume of nectar that had been collected in just a couple of hours. Everyone was working hard—from the pickers, to the transporters, to the packers back at the hive. There was not one pair of idle, unproductive hands; both the bees and the ants were giving their best efforts. By late afternoon, the two communities had collected record amounts of nectar, surpassing everyone's highest expectations.

At the end of the day the bees flew all the ants back to the anthill before they returned to the hive. Belinda was among the last of the bees to leave the anthill, as she first ensured that all of the ants had been safely returned to the anthill. Thanking the general and all of the other ants for their help, she headed back to the hive.

"Successful leaders know that they have to depend on their ability to move from independence to interdependence, from control to connection, from competition to collaboration, from individual to group, and from tight alliances to global networks.

Connective leaders can balance individuality and community."

Episode Six

Everyone was still hard at work storing the collected nectar away for processing when Belinda arrived back at the hive. She was relieved that she would be able to give a glowing report to the queen in their upcoming meeting. But first she went to see how things were going at the nectar processing and honey manufacturing chambers.

As soon as Belinda entered the two adjoined processing and manufacturing chambers, she could see that the working bees were overwhelmed by the sheer volume of nectar that had to be processed and manufactured. They simply couldn't keep up with the huge amount of work that was suddenly expected of them. Belinda frowned as she walked through the two chambers, trying to think of a way to lighten their workload. The problem was that only a specific kind of bee could work there. Manufacturing honey was an extremely intricate process. In addition, it was also the bees' most highly guarded secret, which meant that only the actual honey manufacturers knew how to process and manufacture the honey. To become a manufacturer you had to meet extremely high requirements, pass a series of tests, and then train for six months.

If she was honest and realistic, Belinda had to face the fact that the honey-shortage problem had not been properly solved after all. But before she got too worked up, she had a word with the manager and got all of the facts in black and white. The manager confirmed her fears—there was no way that the manufacturers would be able to process all of the nectar and turn it into honey before the larvae hatched.

BEING HONEST AND REALISTIC

=

QUALITIES OF GOOD LEADERS

The bees were back where they'd started, with an unsolved problem and thousands of hungry mouths to feed. The future of the hive seemed dark and gloomy, without even the slightest ray of hope lingering on the horizon.

With her heart trembling in her shoes, Belinda left the manufacturing chambers and went to see the queen. She wished that she could give her only good news, but she had too much integrity to keep quiet about her discovery. Again, she arrived at the royal egg chamber to find the queen busy laying eggs. Again, this made the queen unavailable to assist with the situation. Again, the queen called upon Belinda to find a solution and save the hive from starvation. Promising the queen for a second time that she would do everything in her power to save the hive, Belinda left the royal egg chamber and returned to her living quarters.

Episode Seven

Belinda was crestfallen. Her heart felt as heavy as a dead star. Falling on her bed, she lay for hours and stared at the ceiling. She didn't have the faintest idea for how to solve the honey problem. Even if they immediately started training more manufacturers, it would still take months before the trainees would be ready to manufacture honey themselves. In the meantime, the hive would be as hungry as ever. No, she needed an immediate solution; she needed to find some way to instantly produce vast quantities of honey, but how?

> **She was going to have to start THINKING OUTSIDE OF THE BOX, BROADEN her perspective, and approach the problem from DIFFERENT ANGLES.**

Belinda realized that if she wanted to find a solution, she was going to have to start thinking outside of the box, broaden her perspective, and approach the problem from different angles. Asking herself all sorts of questions, Belinda gave her mind free reign and allowed it to go beyond her normal, conventional way of thinking. In the process, a spark of genius hit her! The solution to the problem lay within the problem itself! The honey had been taken from the hive to be packaged and sold in large quantities in the human world. All she needed to do was purchase honey from the human shops!

Buzzing with excitement, Belinda started drawing up a strategic plan to secure large amounts of honey from the human shops. She examined every aspect of the process, from the purchase of the honey, to feeding the hive and larvae, to storing away the surplus. She knew that David would help her to buy the honey, but they would still need money for the purchase.

The more time Belinda spent thinking things through, considering every aspect of the task at hand, the clearer she became about what needed to be done and how to accomplish that objective. She had a well-defined vision of abundance for the hive, and every decision and plan she was making was designed to get them closer to that vision. Using everything she had learned from the general, she drew up a full set of plans that depicted every step of the process. She then assigned roles to a couple of key bees, and then set goals and deadlines for everyone. With a full, glorious set of plans drawn up, Belinda climbed into bed and fell into a peaceful sleep, happy in the knowledge that she would be able to save the hive after all.

Belinda was up before dawn the next morning. She had a zillion things to do that day, but first she went to see the queen. The queen was delighted with Belinda's plan and sent her away with instructions to proceed immediately. Heading out of the hive, Belinda hurriedly set off in the direction of David's house. The success of her plan revolved entirely around him and his cooperation. Since bees don't possess human money, she had to draw up a full proposal describing how they would compensate him should he decide to purchase the honey for them. She felt excited about her plan, and was sure that David would agree to help them after he had heard her proposal. Just in time, Belinda arrived just as David was climbing in his car to go to work.

"Good morning, Belinda! And where are you flying to so early in the morning?" David greeted Belinda with a friendly smile as she landed on his steering wheel.

"Good morning, David!" Belinda felt confident and well prepared for the conversation about to take place. The vision and the goals she had for the hive were so clear in her mind that she could almost touch them. "I'm so glad that I caught you before you headed off to work," she smiled, making herself a little more comfortable.

"Oh? And why is that?" David asked.

"I've come to see you because the farmer wouldn't negotiate with me." Belinda went on to tell him everything that had happened since the last time they had seen each other. "Now, I've managed to come up with another plan to save the hive, but it'll require some help from you." Belinda looked David straight in the eyes.

"You know I'll always help where I can," David said supportively. "What do you need?"

"As I've said, we need large quantities of processed honey," Belinda explained. "The only place you can find such large quantities for sale is in human shops."

"So you need me to buy some for your hive," David smiled. "That's not a problem. How much do you need?"

Belinda then went on to describe her plan. Finally she concluded, "To compensate you for buying the honey, we'll keep your garden pest free for the rest of the summer, as well as giving you ten milliliters of honey for the next six months. How does that sound?"

"Of course I'll help you, but I don't want to be compensated in any way. Let's just call it a gift between friends," David said. "Belinda, I must say that you've grown into quite a leader. I'm proud of you for not giving up on this."

"Thank you, David. You don't know how much it means to hear that, especially coming from you." Belinda cheeks burned. She felt quite shy in the face of such praise.

"I'll have the honey ready for you when I get home after work. Should I drop it off at the hive?" David put his keys into the car's ignition.

"Yes, if you don't mind, that would be great. Thank you so much for all of your help!" Belinda's heart was singing. "I'll see you this afternoon, then!" Belinda watched him start his car and reverse out of his driveway before she flew out of the window and headed back to the hive, ecstatic.

ARE YOU A HELPER?

Episode Eight

Back at the hive, Belinda sent messenger bees out to summon all of the bees for a meeting. They had a lot to do before David arrived with the honey. While the messenger bees were busy assembling all the bees, Belinda went to share the good news with the queen. The queen was overjoyed and gave Belinda carte blanche to do whatever she thought necessary to successfully execute her plan.

Belinda was high on life when she left the queen's chamber. Her whole body seemed to be vibrating with vigor, joy, and vitality. She had never felt so alive! Things were finally turning around for her. For the first time ever, she felt as though she was living up to her potential. She couldn't wait to set her plan into action and become fully operational.

Securing the honey was only the first step of a much larger plan—she had another joker up her sleeve.

A little while later, walking up to the podium in the community hall, Belinda looked around at the thousands of anxious faces, all waiting breathlessly to hear what she had to say. Excitement bubbled through her veins like expensive champagne. Her enthusiasm swept over her fellow bees as she addressed them and broadly explained her entire plan and what it involved. She confidently clarified every aspect of her plan, and then delegated tasks to a key group of bees, dividing the rest of the workers into other groups to perform various tasks. Even though David had said that he didn't want any compensation for buying the honey, Belinda still assigned groups of workers to pollinate the flowers in his garden and to rid his garden of all the pests that were eating away at his flowers. The remaining groups of workers were sent out to gather nutshells. They would use these to scoop the honey from the container and transport it to the larvae's compartments, filling each compartment with enough honey to feed the hungry larvae that would soon be hatching.

After the meeting, Belinda was pleased to see everything going exactly as planned with everyone working together in effective and efficient harmony. By the time that David arrived with the honey, all of the preparations had been made and the bees were ready to scoop and transport the honey to the larvae's compartments. The surplus honey was to be divided—some of it had to be used for the feast Belinda had organized for that evening, while the rest was to be used to feed the hive over the next couple of weeks. After all, they were going to be so busy that Belinda feared that there wasn't going to be enough time to collect and process any other nectar.

As she surveyed the end results of her plan, Belinda was proud of the hive and everything they had accomplished together. Against all odds they had managed to secure enough honey to feed both the larvae and themselves for a couple of weeks. But even though Belinda was extremely proud of all of them, she still wasn't completely satisfied with their situation in the hive. She felt that there was still a lot more work to do before she would officially dare to say that the hive had been saved.

> **WHEN YOU LOOK AT THE RESULTS IN YOUR LIFE, DO YOU FEEL PROUD OF EVERYTHING YOU HAVE ACCOMPLISHED?**

To reward everyone for the hard work done, Belinda organized a huge feast for the next day. She invited the ants to take part in the celebrations, and, together, the ants and the bees celebrated from early the next morning until late in the afternoon—drinking honey, dancing merrily, and socializing like old friends. Belinda took part in some of the festivities, but she couldn't fully enjoy herself; her mind was preoccupied with securing and safeguarding the future of the hive.

> **"REWARD EVERYONE FOR THE HARD WORK DONE, INCLUDING YOUR OWN!"**

By midafternoon, while everyone else was still having a good time, Belinda went to see the queen, who was surprised that Belinda wasn't celebrating with the rest of the bees. Belinda elaborately explained the plan she had concocted to safeguard the future of the hive. The queen was overcome by admiration and appreciation for the foresight Belinda was displaying, and she immediately gave her blessing for the implementation of Belinda's plan.

With the queen's blessing, Belinda went to visit David, and once again she asked him for his help. In Belinda's eyes, the fact that vast amounts of honey had been procured didn't automatically guarantee the secure future of the hive. Belinda felt herself responsible to ensure that the hive would never again find itself in such a dire situation. She was hoping for the best, but planning for the worst. She had considered all sorts of different scenarios that could threaten the hive's future wellbeing, and had drawn up a set of prevention plans to safeguard the hive should any of those scenarios take place in the future. Now she was on her way to see David with a mutually beneficial proposition that would create a safe and secure future for the hive.

"Belinda! Hi!" David was busy watering the flowers in his garden.

"Hi there, David!" Belinda buzzed over the grass, touched down on top of the patio table, and watched David finish watering his flowers.

"You've really been busy these last couple of days," David said as he joined her, making himself comfortable on one of the patio chairs.

"Yes, I'm pretty tired. The honey crises really kept me quite busy this week," Belinda answered. "The problem is that we're not completely out of the woods yet."

"What do you mean? Do you need me to get you some more honey?" David sounded confused.

"No, no, you brought more than enough honey to feed the larvae and the rest of the hive for weeks to come," Belinda quickly assured him. "I'm talking about the safe future of the hive. I did some scenario planning, and it has become clear to me that we'll have to take certain precautionary measures to prevent the hive from ever finding itself in such a horrible situation again."

"Now, that's using your brain!" David was impressed by the growth of his little bee friend over the last couple of days. "What are you thinking of doing to prevent such a disaster from happening in the future?"

"The obvious answer would be to make sure that we always have surplus amounts of honey available, right? The problem is that we can't store extra honey in the hive. If we did, the farmer would just remove it when he was collecting. We have to find a secure place away from the hive where we can store our honey. It has to be a place where no one, not the farmer or anyone else, can remove it and leave us dying of hunger again."

Belinda moved closer to the edge of the patio table as she spoke. She wanted to be able to look David properly in the eye when she made her proposal.

"Good thinking," David praised her. "Have you found a place?"

"Well, that's why I'm here," Belinda said, confident in her offer. "Your garden shed would be the perfect place. So I wanted to find out if you would consider renting a section of your shed to us. We would only need a small corner to erect a storage hive, and, in return, once a month we'll give you ten percent of the honey we store away in your shed. What do think?"

"Of course you can store the honey away in my shed!" David answered without hesitation, giving his little bee friend a big smile.

"Thank you so much, David, I knew I could count on you!" Belinda said warmly. Filled with excitement, she went on to explain that they would initially only build a small storage hive in the shed. But her plans didn't end there. She wanted the bees to break free from the farmer's tyranny for good. Ultimately, she wanted the bees to develop and expand the storage hive into a fully developed hive. Then, in time, they would move their entire community into the hive in the shed, forever ridding them of the farmer's unjustly ways.

When Facing Challenges its Always GOOD to Have Someone to Count on!

"Wow, Belinda, you should be really proud of yourself! You've turned into quite the effective leader. The queen can count herself lucky to have you on her side." David was amazed with the progress his friend had made in such a short period of time. "Come on, let's go to the shed and clear some space for your hive." David headed off towards the shed.

ARE YOU PROUD
OF YOURSELF?

WHAT CAN YOU DO
TO KEEP BEING

PROUD OF YOURSELF?

Episode Ten

(End of the Beginning!)

Back at the hive Belinda called the queen and all of her fellow bees together for a meeting. Since she was still laying eggs, the queen was carried in on her bed and placed next to Belinda's podium. Everyone was still in good spirits from the celebration and they all enthusiastically listened to the plans that Belinda had made for their future. It was while she was standing on the podium addressing the hive that Belinda realized for the first time that she was beginning to fulfill her dreams of achieving more with her life. The honey crisis had forced her to start using her dormant potential. She had grown from a humble worker into an effective leader, a leader who everyone was looking to for guidance, inspiration, and advice.

> **"The honey crisis had forced Belinda to start using her dormant potential. She had grown from a humble worker into an effective leader, a leader who everyone was looking to for guidance, inspiration, and advice."**

It's so important to remember that *anyone can achieve anything* they set their mind to. Belinda didn't just suddenly turn into a great leader, the potential was always there, she simply had to work at developing the potential she already had, and channel it in the right direction. *Leaders are made, not born.* We all have the necessary potential to become effective leaders, we merely need to learn how to develop and hone that potential. In the process, we can grow into effective leaders, using courage, focus, humility, integrity, clarity, dependability, and foresight to lead those around us.

> **You are the Master of Your Life. It's time to take control and lead yourself to a better future.**

Now that we are at the conclusion of Belinda's story, ask yourself:

What is my life story?

Am I writing the story of my life?

Or Am I letting others writing the story of my life?

You are unique!

You are the only one who can write the real story of your life? Take action now and start today writing the story of your life....

"It's been said that the best way to teach is through a story and this book re-emphasizes my believe in the saying. The quality and yet simple words in use are a testament to the author's intelligent thinking, the easy read of the book cuts across all age groups.
The message is simple and clear; 'the limit to what we can achieve is in our mind'.
Thank you Ailson for the encouragement within this rich book."

--- Hannah Fredrick
Legalframes, UK

Episode Eleven

(It's my time now!)

This is the true version of the story of my life…..

PS. Share your story with the author, please contact me at www.whereismyhoney.com - I would be delighted to read your story ☺. Ailson J. De Moraes

Share It With Others

Available in hardcopy and E-Copy

www.whereismyhoney.com

10% of the sales profit of this book and All Ailson's services, including keynote speeches and seminars are dedicated to De Moraes Foundation.

For more information, go to www. ailsondemoraes.com

Help your people to find their *'honey'* and build a truly successful organization

FOR MORE INFORMATION ON KEYNOTE SPEECHES AND SEMINARS GO TO <u>WWW. WHEREISMYHONEY.COM</u>

"There is no doubt that attending one of Ailson's talks will get you thinking about life and the way things impact you and more importantly how you impact society. Ailson style of presentation is interactive and incredibly warming!"

--- Fizza Malik

Whatever stage of our lives we are, we all share something in common: *a need to find our 'honey' and succeed in changing times.* In the end of the day, we are all the same; *we are all humans looking for 'honey'.*

To Your Mastery,

Ailson J. De Moraes

Synopsis

Ailson is a Human Behavioural Scientist, Philanthropist, Author, University Teacher and International Speaker who is on a mission, one that has led him and his unique art of Leadership and Creativity throughout South and North America, Europe, Africa and Asia. People from every corner of the globe have praised him as being a *"highly knowledgeable and inspirational speaker"*. As an international speaker, Ailson has spoken to a variety of audiences from executives, to professional teachers, to teenagers and even to primary school teachers and students. His simple but powerful approach has helped him to be welcomed by any age group of creative minds around the world.

Where is My Honey? is an Simple Tale about Achieving our Goals and Ambitions by Adapting our Circumstances in Life. It is not just a story about bees and honey; it is an opportunity to reflect on your capacities. Our goals and ambitions change all the time and we need to change with the time. If we are not adaptable to the changes we face along our life journey, we may become extinct like dinosaurs. We come to cross roads in our lives all the time. We need to adapt and determine to be comfortable with the road we take. If we are not adaptable to the changes we will sit on the cross roads without going anywhere. **Remember, Success in Life comes with, Determination, Adaptation and the Changes you decided to make it. While reading this little but powerful story of a simple bee I invite you to reflect in your professional and personal life. Think where you are in your life? Are you achieving your goals and ambitions? Where do you want to be in the next five, ten or even fifteen years?**

"A great story! I enjoyed reading it! It was a pleasant way to learn about leadership. I agree that leaders can be made."

--- Laura Migenda, Deloitte

"This book is unique, in the sense that it is simple to understand but holds a powerful message.

I highly recommend this book if anyone wants a simple insight into leadership and motivation.

Read this book!"

--- Crystal Ho, KPMG

"This accessible and thought-provoking story reminds us of the links between the values of teamwork, hard-work and leadership.

I found it both inspiring and beneficial, and shall be using it to convey its positive message to others."

--- Dr Chris Bonnici, University of Malta

The quality and yet simple words in use are a testament to the author's intelligent thinking, the easy read of the book cuts across all age groups. The message is simple and clear; 'the limit to what we can achieve is in our mind'.

Thank you Ailson for the encouragement within this rich book."

--- Hannah Fredrick, UK